SWAMPS
and
MARSHES

Troll Associates

SWAMPS
and
MARSHES

by Francene Sabin

Illustrated by Barbara Flynn

Troll Associates

Library of Congress Cataloging in Publication Data

Sabin, Francene.
   Swamps and marshes.

   Summary: Explains how swamps and marshes are formed,
describes the plants and animals that live in them, and
discusses the importance of wetlands in nature's overall
pattern.
   1. Marshes—Juvenile literature.   2. Swamps—Juvenile
literature. [1. Marshes.   2. Swamps.   3. Ecology]
I. Flynn, Barbara, ill.   II. Title.
GB621.S24   1985   574.5′26325   84-2717
ISBN 0-8167-0280-2 (lib. bdg.)
ISBN 0-8167-0281-0 (pbk.)

From a distance, the swamps and marshes look silent and deserted. But move closer... watch and listen closely...and you will discover a world of activity.

Soft breezes rustle the wetland grasses. A dragonfly turns in midair to capture a mosquito in flight. A green heron swoops to a gentle landing and pokes its long beak into the water. A moment later, the heron brings up a small fish and gulps it down. Frogs sing a croaking chorus. The air is filled with the hum of insects, the honking of passing geese, and the sharp cries of a red-winged blackbird.

The wetlands are nurseries of life. Each day they give birth to countless living things. Plants, insects, birds, fish, frogs, turtles, snakes, and mammals are born here and nourished in this rich environment. The wetlands tell a story of life that has been going on for millions of years.

There are three main kinds of wetlands —bogs, marshes, and swamps. A bog is the simplest of the three. Most bogs were once ponds or small lakes, but they became choked with plant life. They are not fed by moving water from rivers or streams, but are almost always locked in on all sides by land.

Landlocked water

Bogs are found in pockets of ground once covered by glacial ice. About ten thousand years ago the glaciers melted. They left behind large holes in the ground, which filled with the water from the melted masses of ice. In time, plants grew and died, and the water became clogged with sediment and dead plant matter.

The formation of a bog starts with clumps of sphagnum moss and other plant matter, covering the top of the landlocked water. The sphagnum moss absorbs huge amounts of water, which it uses to grow. When the moss dies, it sinks to the bottom and piles up as layers of a substance called peat. After years of this process, the pond has turned into a spongy peat bog.

A marsh is an area of wet, spongy land dotted with pools of water. Plants and animals of many kinds are found in marshes. The plants that grow here are mostly grasses and reeds. The kinds of grasses and reeds found in a particular marsh depend on where the marsh is located.

Inland fresh-water marshes in cool climates contain bulrushes, cattails, wild rice, and many kinds of grasses. Inland freshwater marshes in warmer climates are home to the pale purple flowers of water hyacinths and the delicate water primroses, in addition to grasses and reeds.

There are also salt marshes, found at the edge of oceans. The plants growing in this type of environment must be able to survive in salt water. In salt marshes, you will find cord grass, salt hay, and a great deal of microscopic plant life known as algae.

Swamps are like marshes in many ways. The major difference is that swamps have trees in addition to grasses and reeds. In most cases, swamp trees grow on small humps of soil that stick up above the swamp waters. But one tree, the mangrove, grows right in swamp water.

The mangrove, which grows in warm-weather swamps like the Florida Everglades, is the only tree in the world that can live in

𝒳.

salt water. Mangrove trees grow close together—so close that their clawlike roots seem to be meshed together in a wooden web.

Mangrove seeds, which look like long string beans, take root easily in the muddy swamp bottom. Each seedling then sends out prop roots that are like small, sturdy underwater stilts. These prop roots grip the muddy bottom and keep the seedling solidly in place.

The mangrove tree is very important to many warm-weather swamps. It is like an enormous apartment building that houses thousands of tenants. Insects and birds live among its shiny green leaves. Frogs and water snakes use the mangrove branches as perches.

Small fish and shellfish live in the water that surrounds the mangrove roots. They feed on bits of green plants and algae that cling to the tree's roots. Larger fish, such as the tarpon, and such wading birds as the egret, feed on the smaller water animals. Much of the life of the southern tidal swamps depends on the existence of the mangrove tree.

Wetlands are always undergoing change. For example, a lake begins to fill in with dead plant and animal matter until it is a small pond. But the change doesn't stop at that point. The pond continues to be filled in until it is a marsh and then a swamp, with trees taking root. At last, after many years, the wetland becomes dry land.

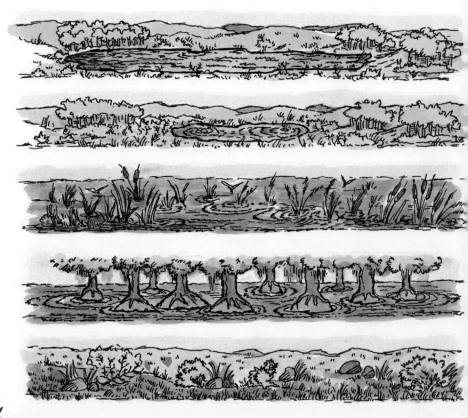

At the same time, new wetlands are being formed, by floods and earthquakes, by erosion, and by a change in direction taken by large bodies of water. In these ways, what was once dry land is turned into wetlands. Grasses take root. Insects, fish, amphibians, reptiles, and birds move in. And the life cycle begins anew.

X

Saltwater tidal marshes can change even more quickly than wetlands located further inland. Tidal marshes form at the ocean's edge, where the land is low. The ocean waves move some of the sand that makes up the coastline. This sand is swept into the shallow waters offshore, where it is dropped. Gradually it builds up until it forms sandbars, or strips of sand.

When sandbars are high enough, they become sandy islands. They protect the coastline by blocking the ocean waves. The low-lying area between the islands and the coastline may eventually become a tidal pool, cut off from the ocean at low tide, but flooded at each high tide.

Tide, wind, and birds carry seeds into this tidal pool. In time, plants take root in the sand beneath the shallow waters. Before long, the tidal pool becomes a full-fledged salt marsh, complete with a wide variety of plant and animal life.

A typical salt marsh along the eastern coast of North America can be home for many kinds of insects, fish, shellfish, birds, and snakes. Mammals, such as raccoons, opossums, and skunks, may also make their homes there. All of these living things are part of a cycle called the food chain.

The food chain begins at the bottom of a salt marsh. There, millions of tiny green plants known as algae become food for worms, crayfish, insects, and other small creatures. Algae are also the main food for oysters, clams, and other shellfish that are found in the mud flats of the tidal marsh.

Fish, such as bluefish, flounder, and striped bass, lay their eggs in the calm waters of the salt marsh. Here, the waves will not harm the eggs, or the fish that hatch from them. Here, too, the young fish will find a good supply of food, in the form of algae and microscopic animal life called plankton. Then, when the fish are large enough to survive in open waters, they will swim out to the ocean at high tide.

Just as young fish depend on the smaller life forms in the marsh, they themselves serve as food for larger fish, for ducks and geese, and for other marsh dwellers. And at the top of the food chain are the mammals. Many raccoons, opossums, and skunks rely on the marsh to supply them with food.

Most people would not find it comfortable to live in a swamp or a marsh. Still, there are some people who choose to make their homes in these places. People live in the Louisiana bayous, the Okefenokee Swamp in Georgia, and the marshes in the mideastern country of Iraq. But these are exceptions.

Swamps and marshes, with their constant dampness and countless insects, have always been forbidding, hostile environments for most humans. For this reason, people used to think of swamps and marshes as useless wastelands. Whenever they could, they drained the swamps of their water, filled in the low-lying land, and built on it.

Only in recent years have we learned just how important our wetlands are. We use the fish and shellfish of the wetlands as food. And even though the mosquitoes that breed in the wetlands are pests, they are necessary food for frogs and toads, snakes and birds—and that makes them important in nature's overall plan. The same is true of nearly every other form of wetlands life.

As we have come to realize how critical the wetlands are, we have increased our efforts to save them. In many countries, wetlands are being set aside as protected areas. In these swamps and marshes, the web of life continues without outside interference.

A frog whips out its sticky tongue and snaps up a passing fly. A heron gulps down another fish and flies off into the distance. And the soft breeze seems to whisper "goodbye" as it rustles the grasses of the peaceful wetland.

PROTECTED
MARSHLAND